Alif Baa
Tracing and Practice

Tip :

You can get even more writing practice by creating reusable sheets!

1. Take this book apart.

    Rip off the cover to more easily tear out its pages.

2. Place individual sheets into sheet protectors.

3. Write on the sheets with dry-erase markers.

4. Wipe off the marker to reuse.

Your opinion matters to us, please do not hesitate to leave a comment on the Amazon website.

ISBN: 9798655673298

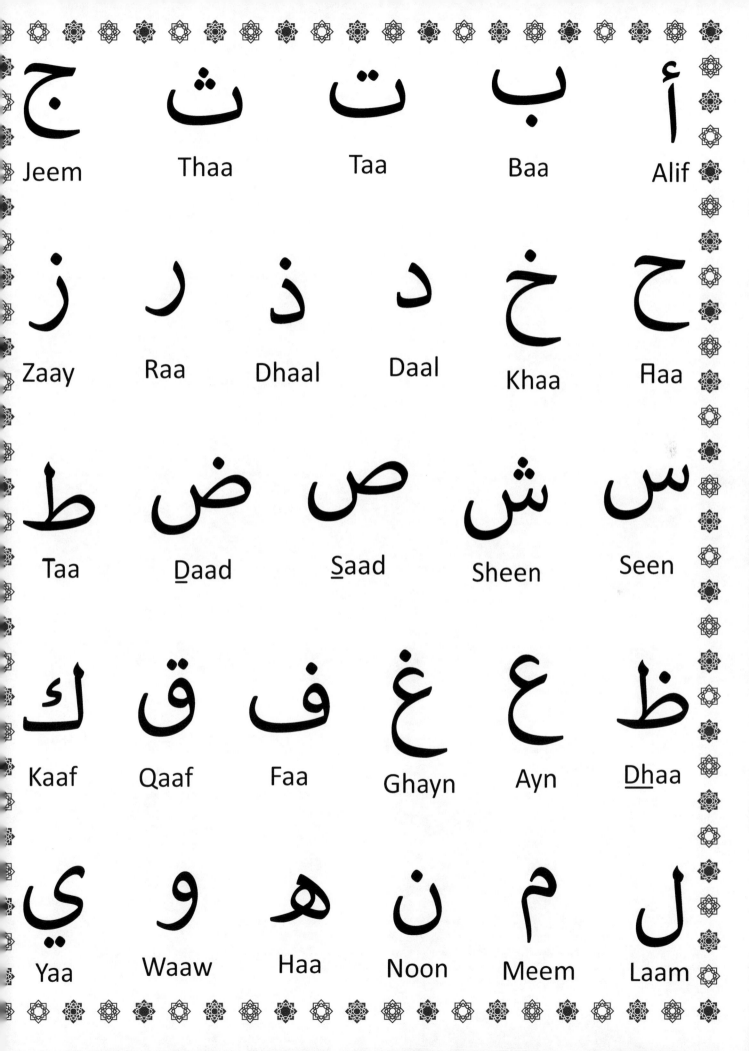

Jeem	Thaa	Taa	Baa	Alif
Zaay	Raa	Dhaal	Daal	Khaa	Ħaa
Taa	<u>D</u>aad	<u>S</u>aad	Sheen	Seen
Kaaf	Qaaf	Faa	Ghayn	Ayn	<u>Dh</u>aa
Yaa	Waaw	Haa	Noon	Meem	Laam

Alif

أَرْنَب

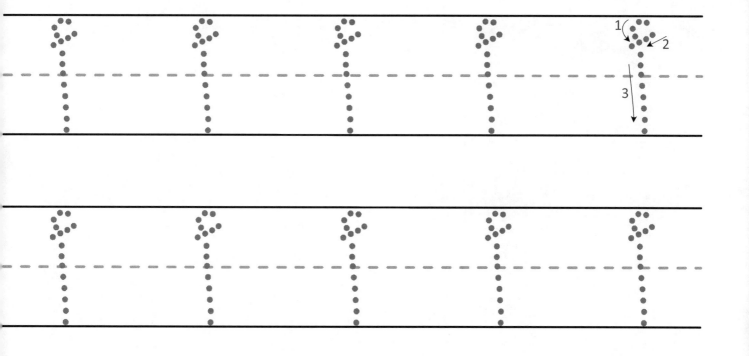

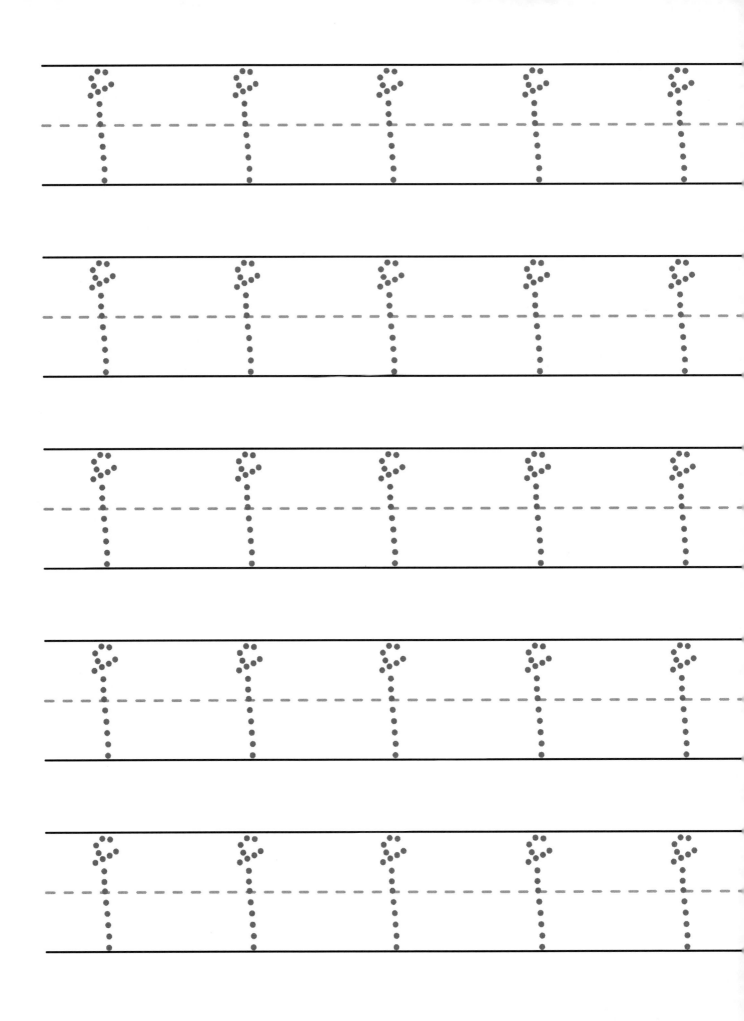

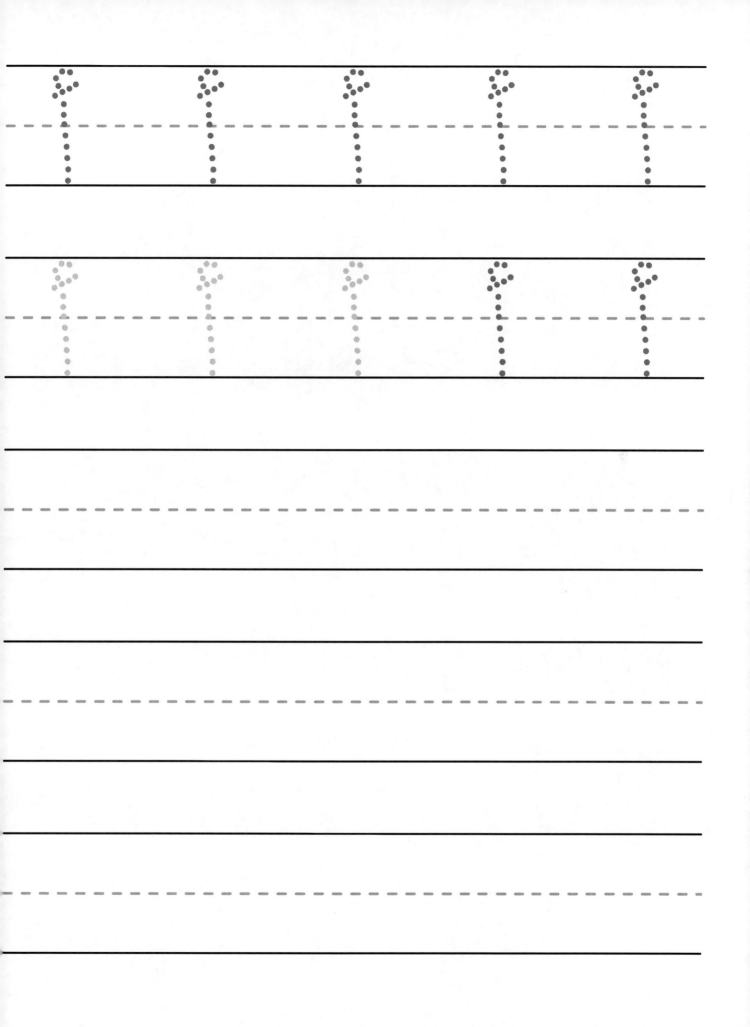

Cow
baqara

Baa

ب

بقرة

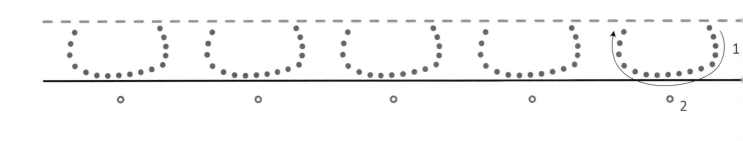

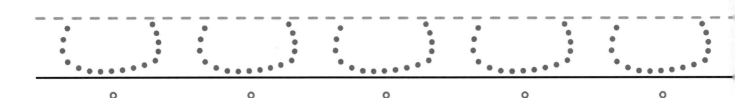

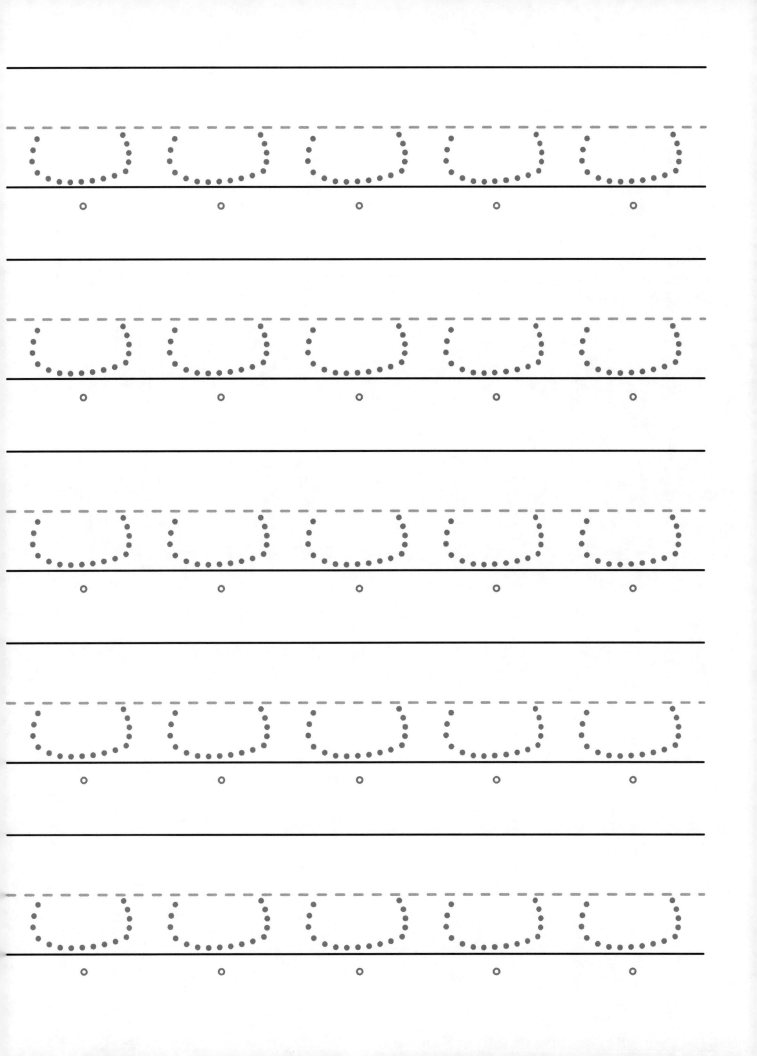

Taa

تفاحة

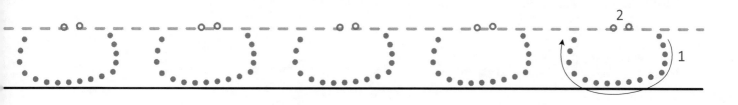

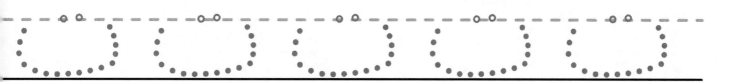

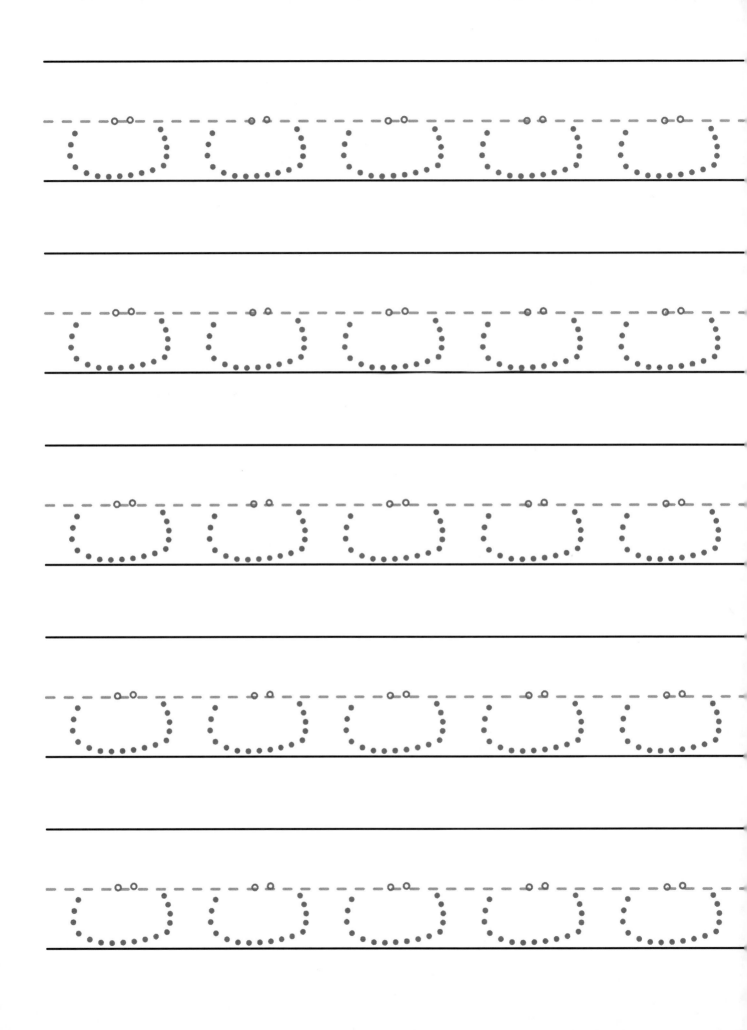

Snake
thueban

Thaa

ثعبان

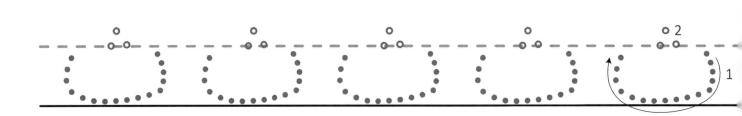

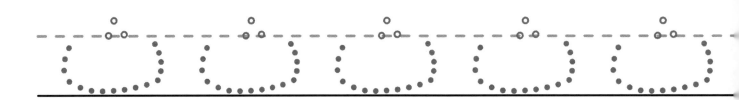

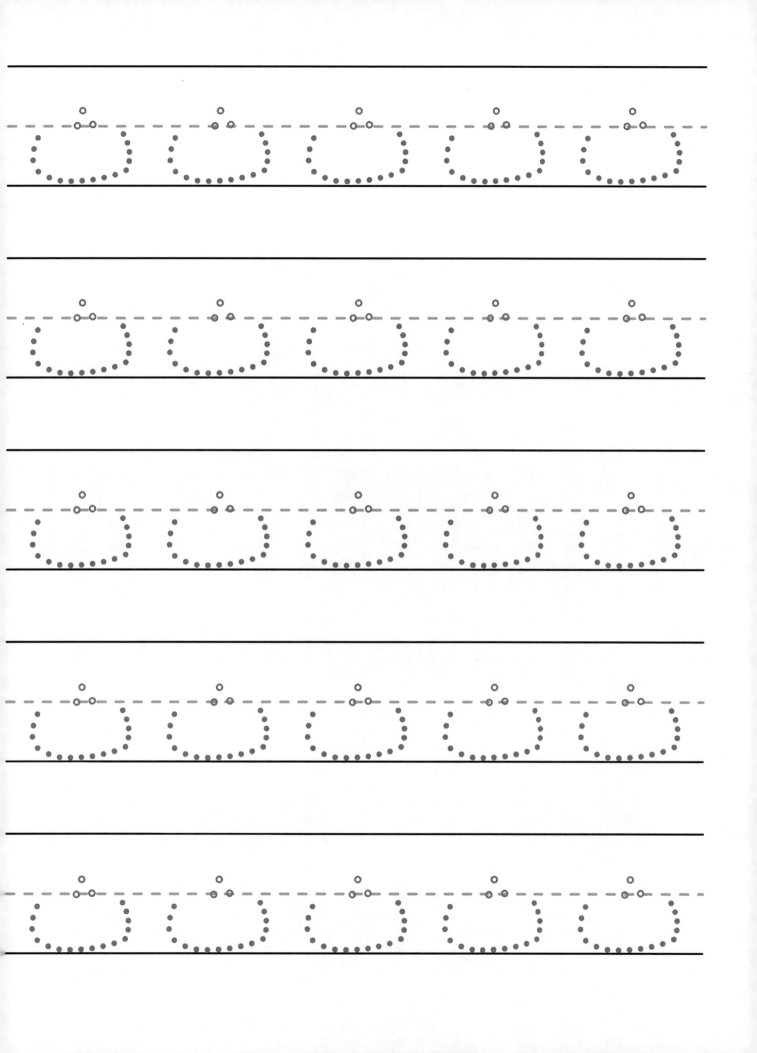

Camel
jamel

Jeem

جمل

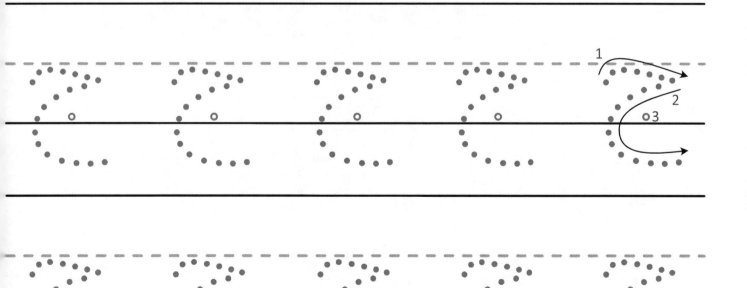

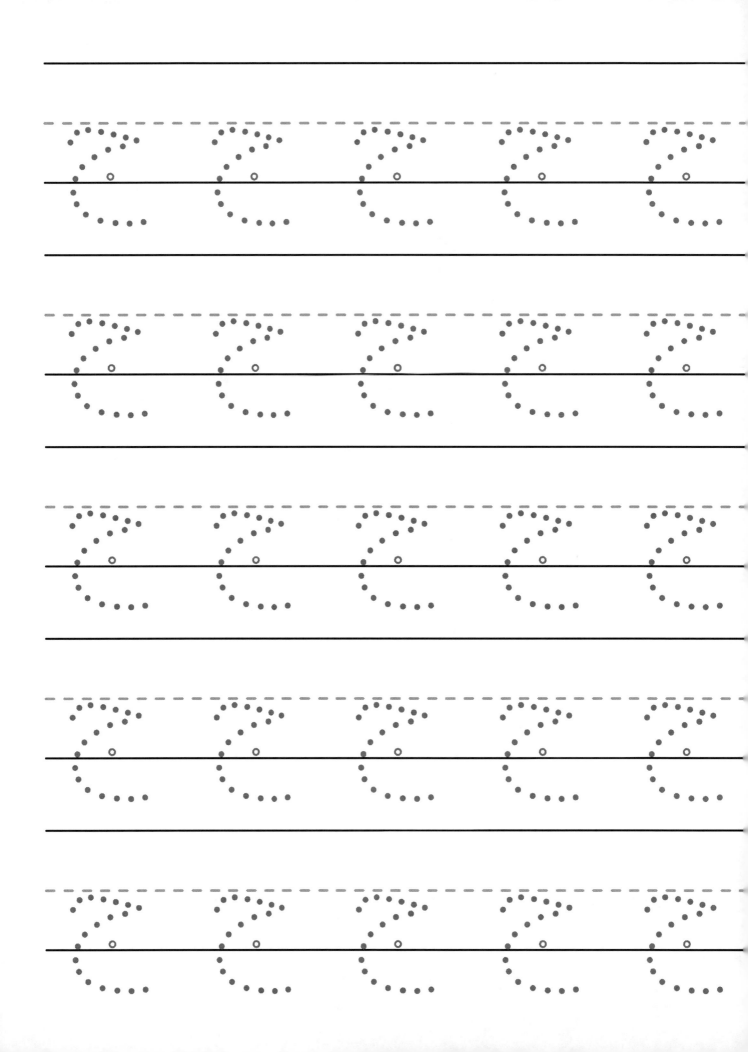

Horse
<u>h</u>isan

حصان

<u>H</u>aa

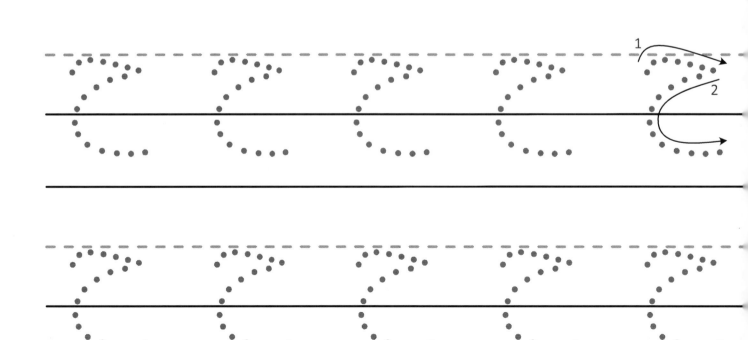

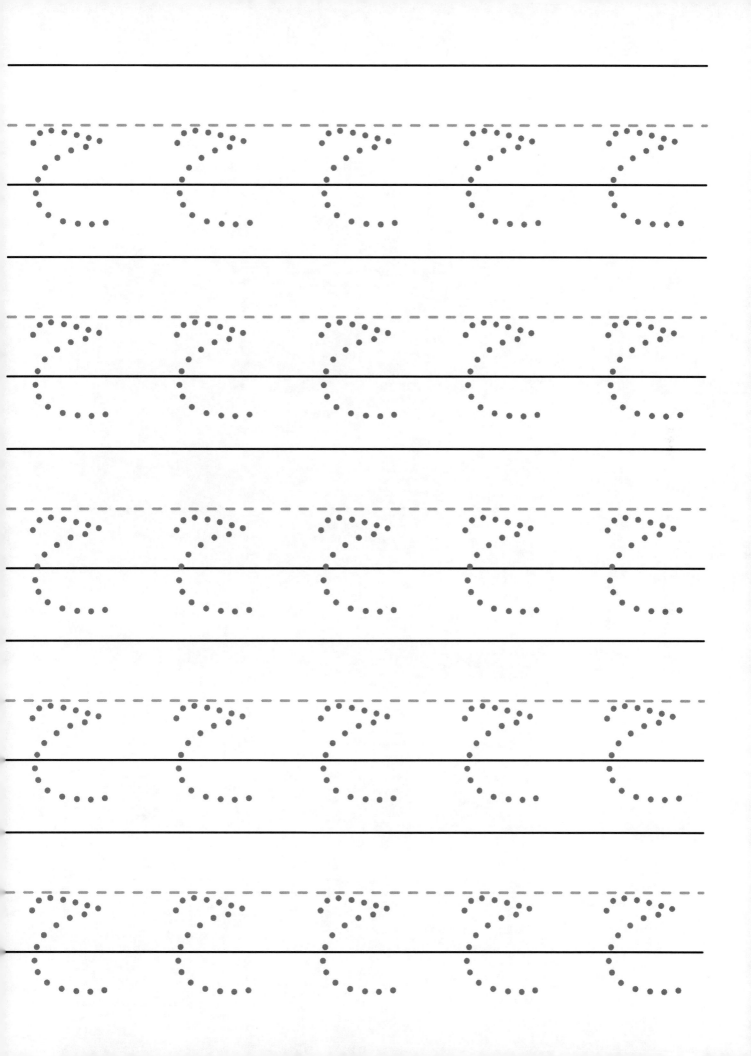

Tent
khayma

Khaa

خيمة

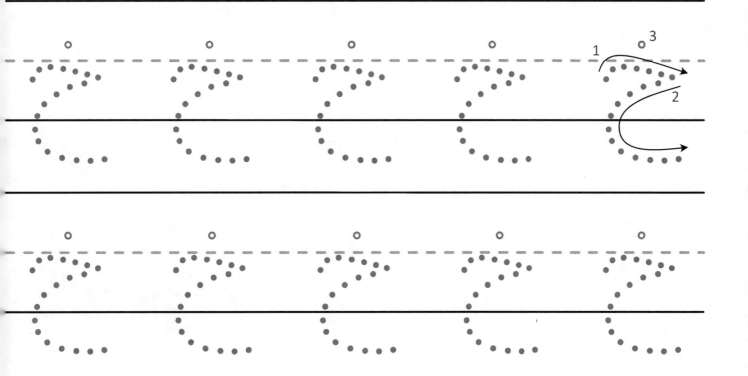

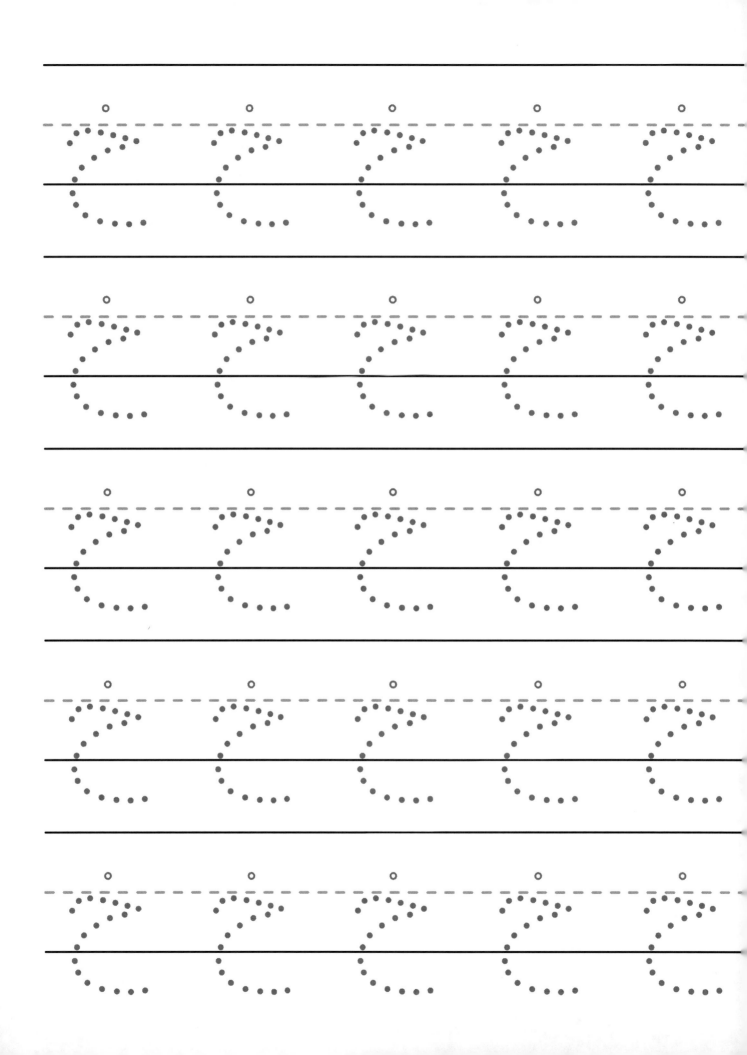

Bear
dub

Daal

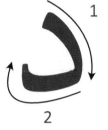

دب

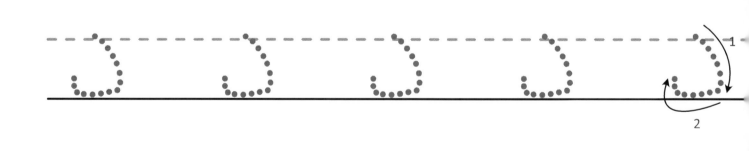

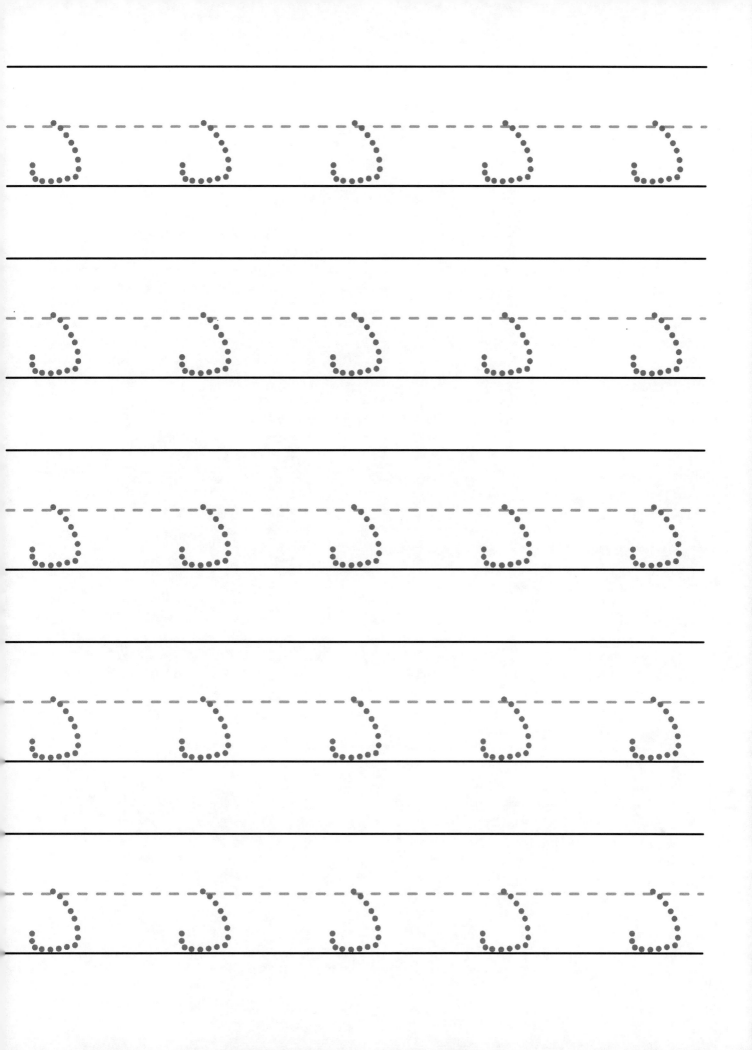

Fly
dhubaba

Dhaal

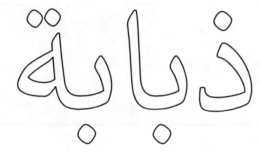

ذبابة

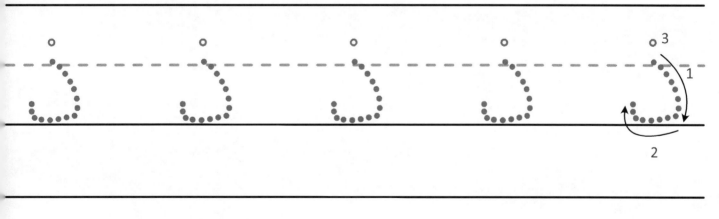

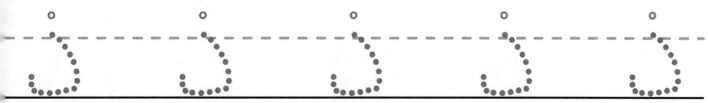

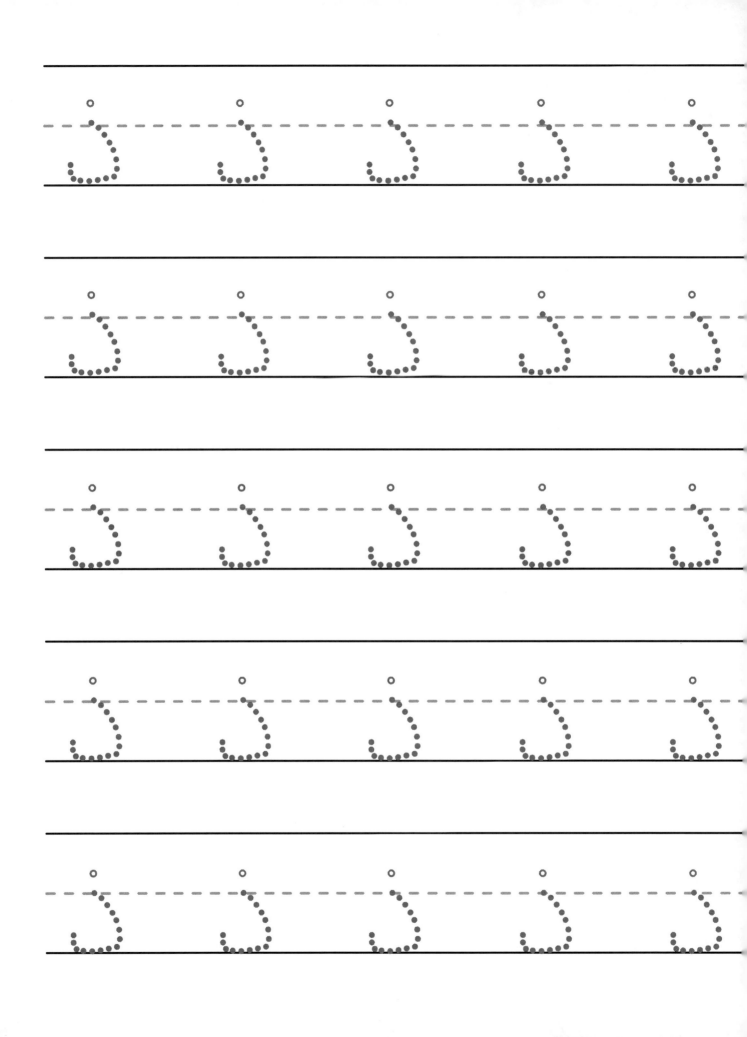

Feather
risha

Raa

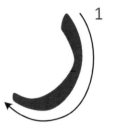

ريشة

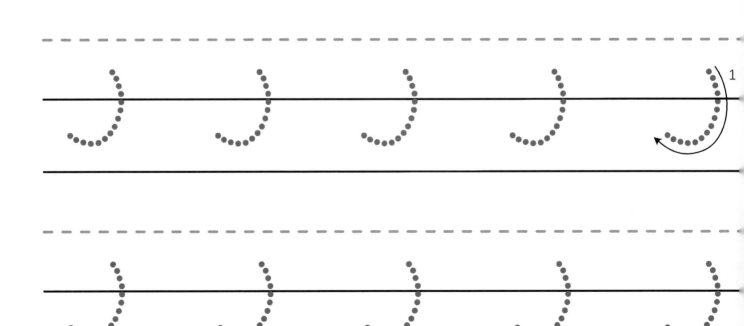

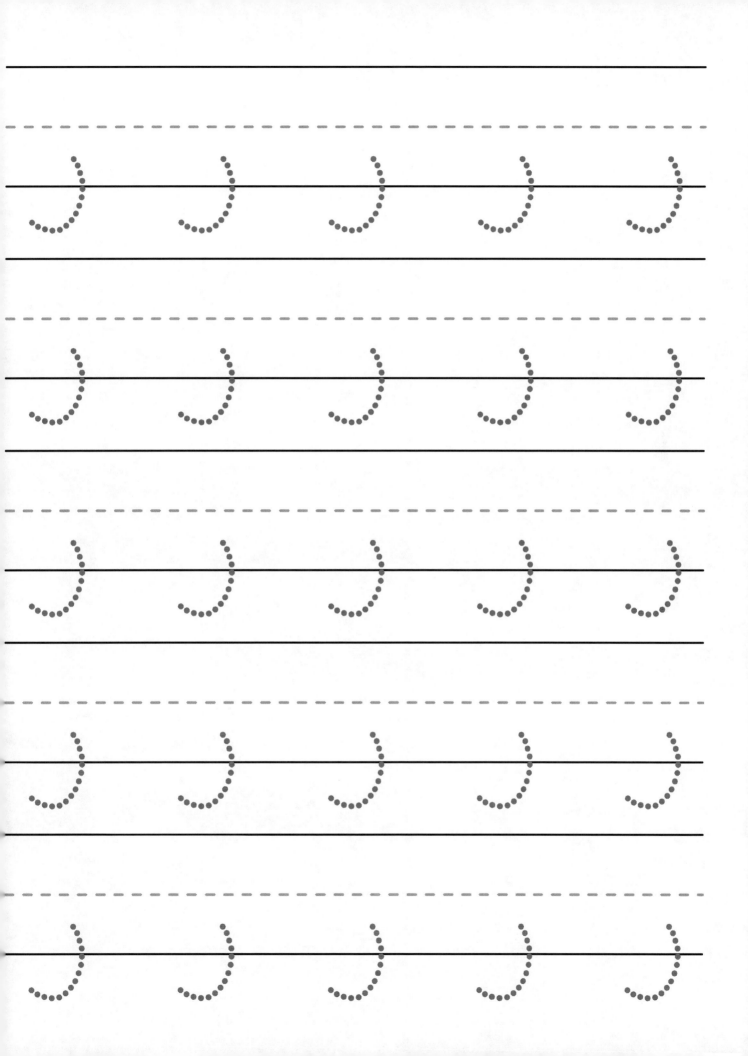

Giraffe
zarafa

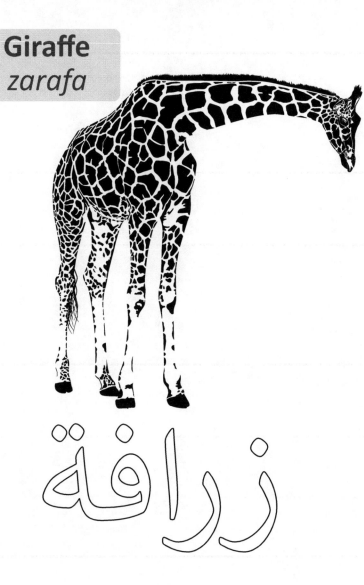

Zaay

زرافة

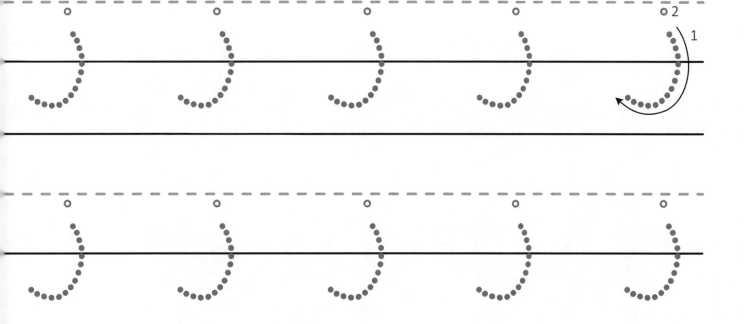

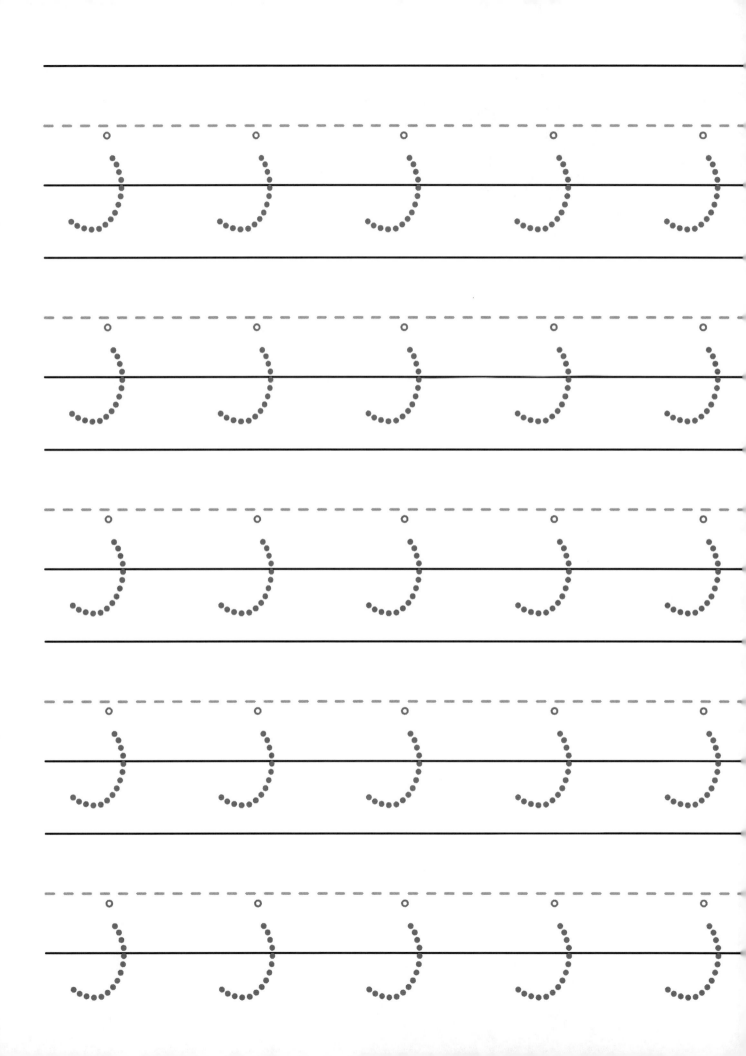

Car
sayara

Seen

سيارة

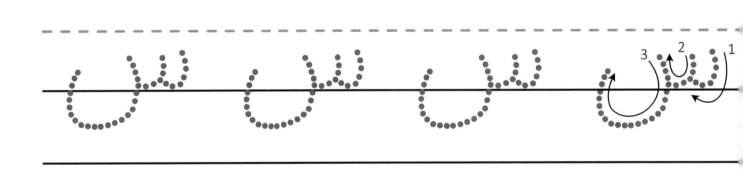

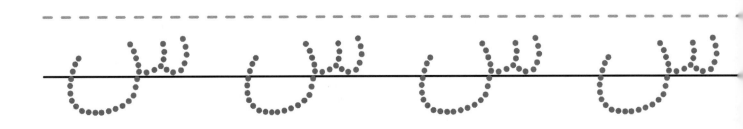

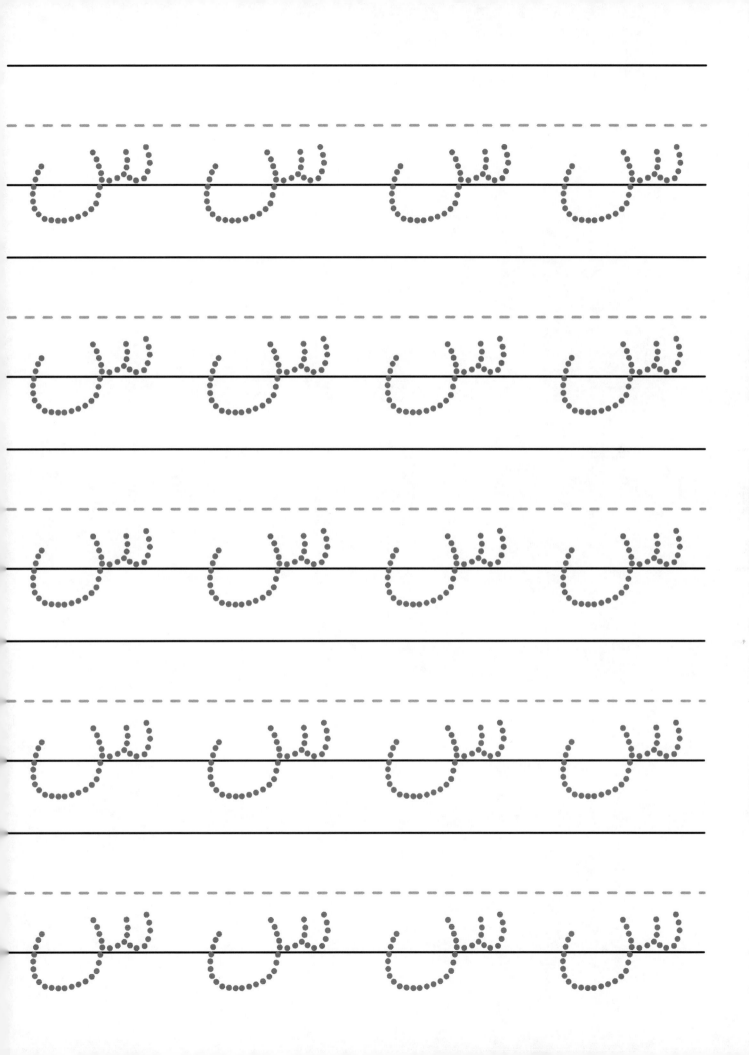

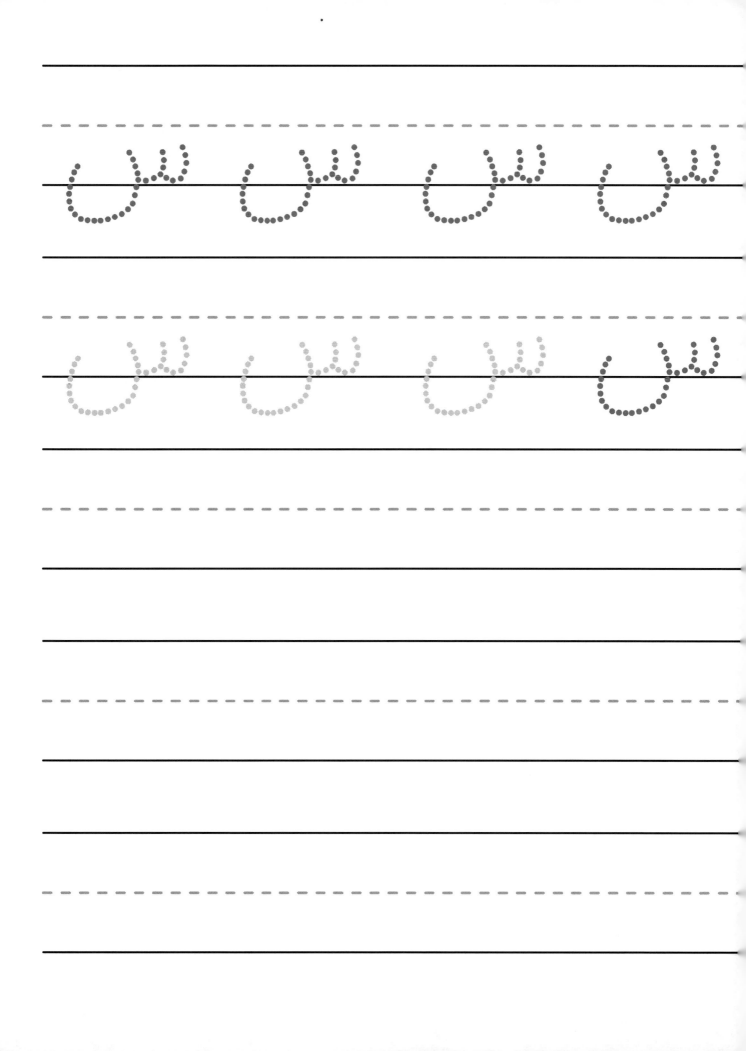

Tree
shajara

Sheen

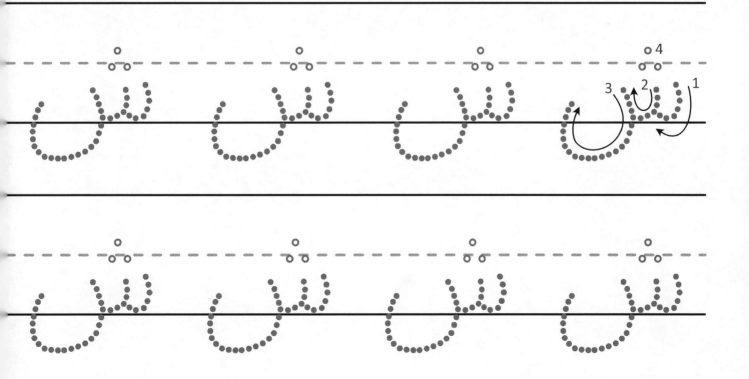

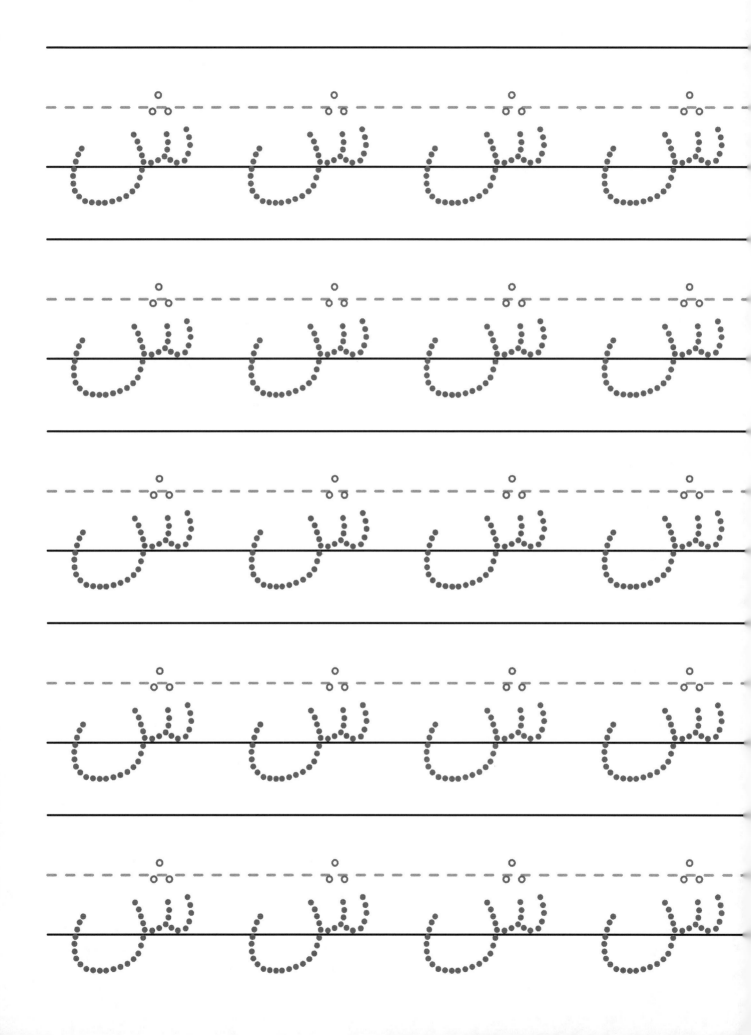

Ṣaad

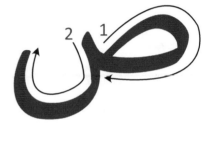

صاروخ

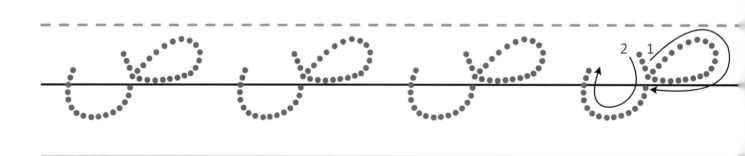

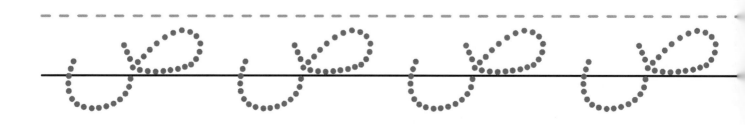

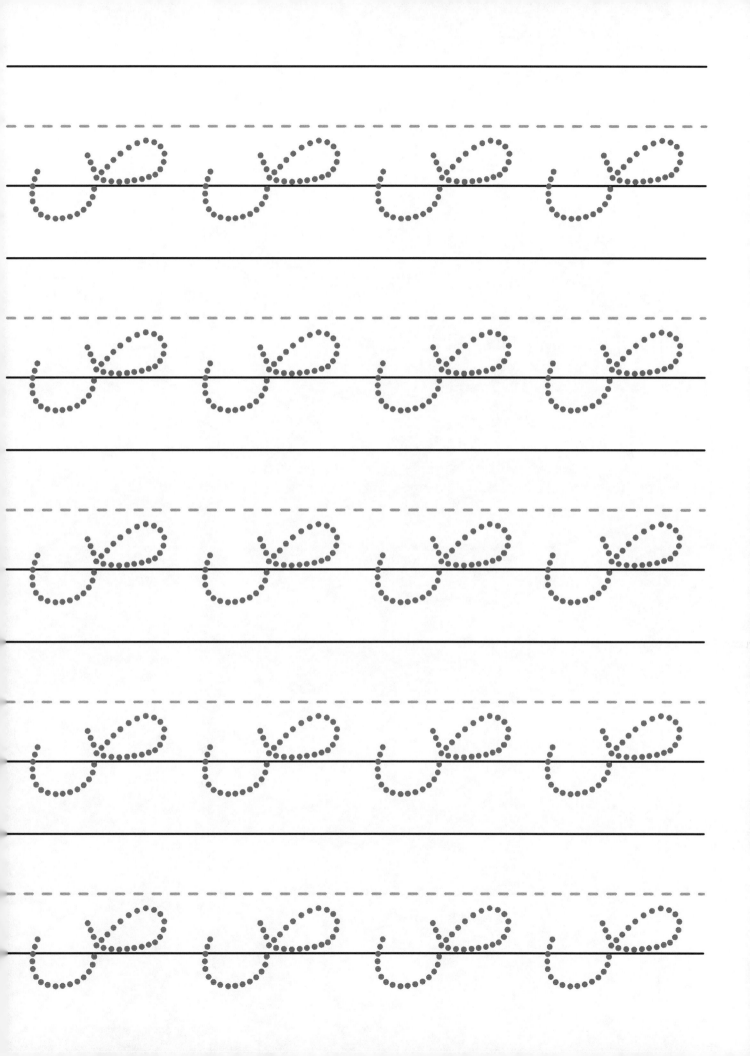

Frog
difdae

Daad

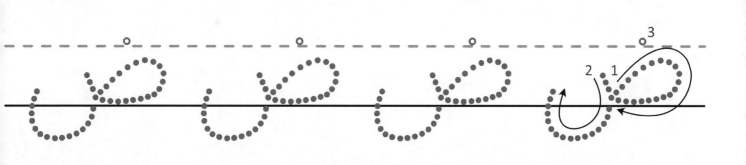

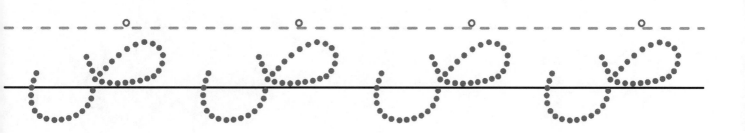

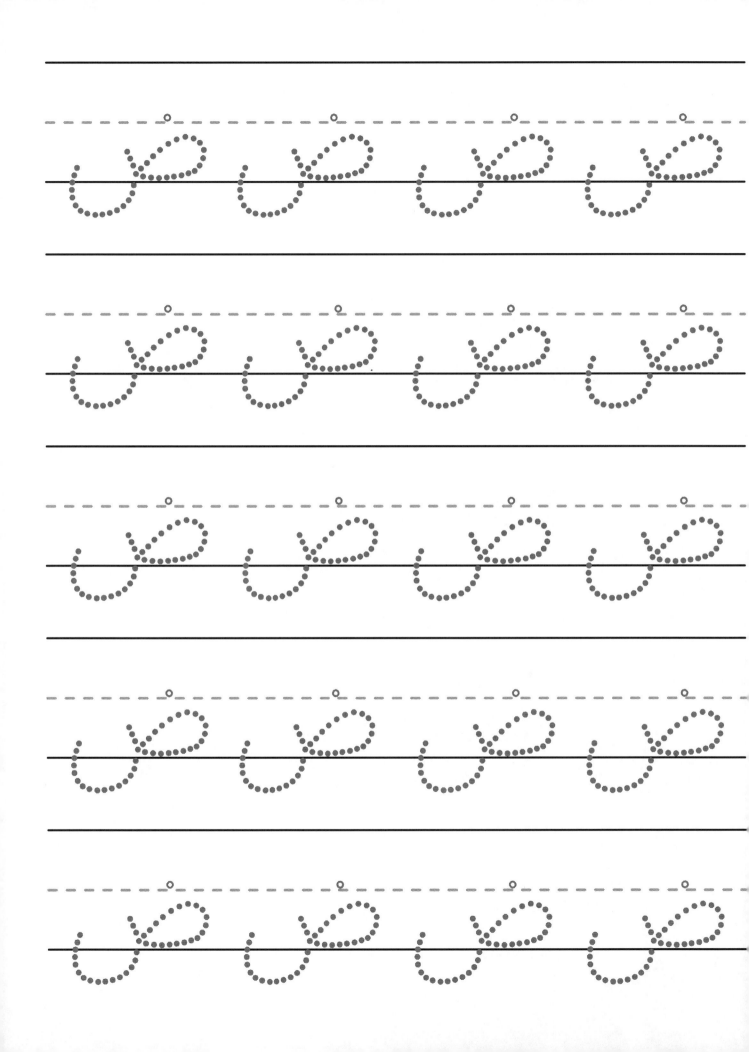

Table
tawila

Taa

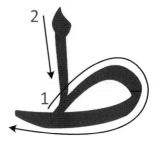

طاولة

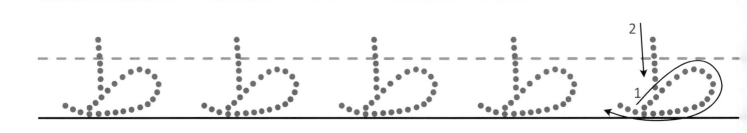

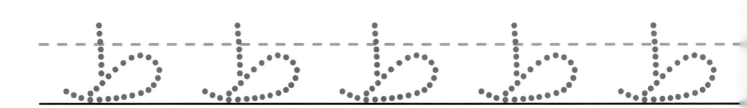

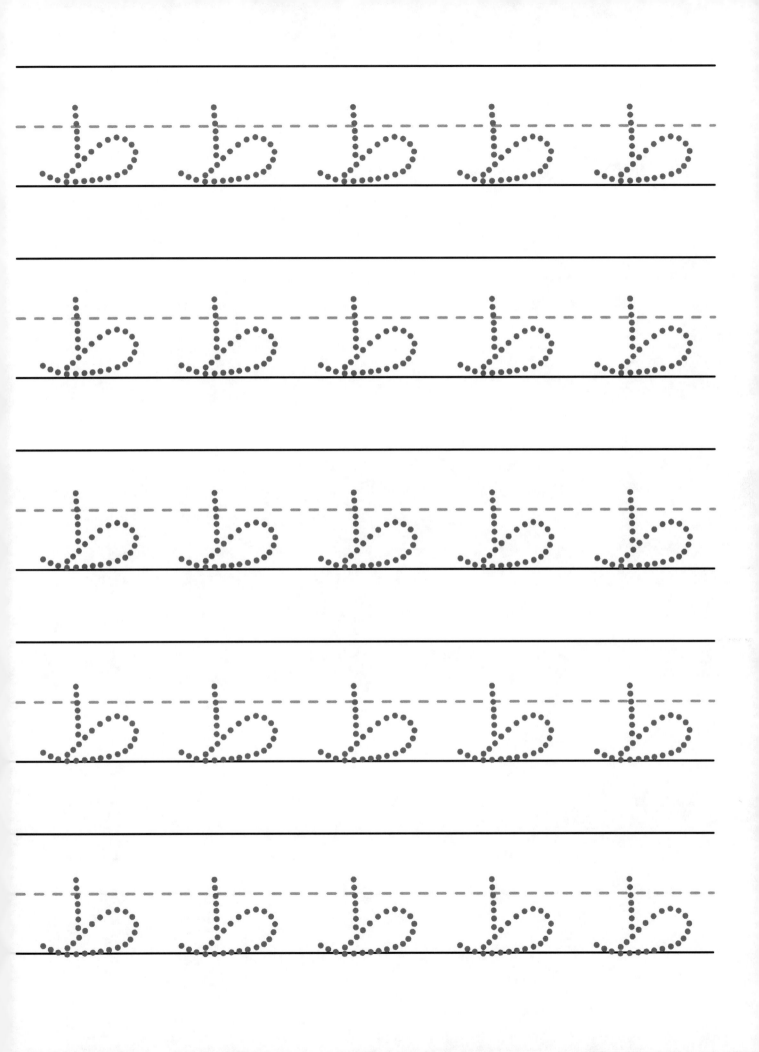

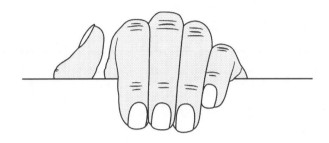

Dhaa

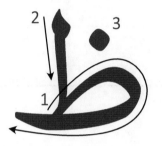

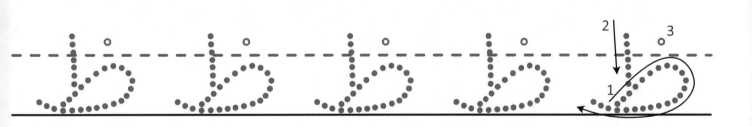

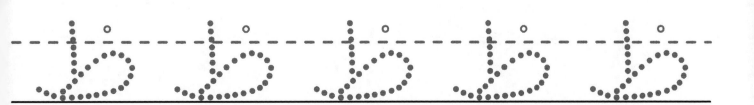

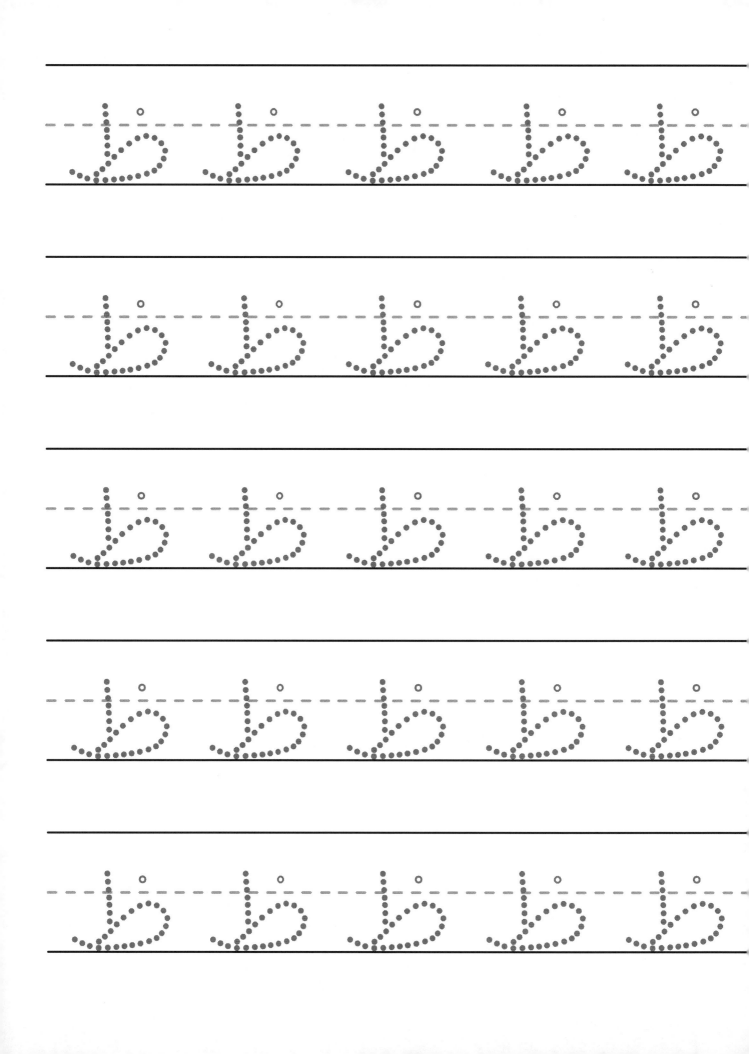

Bird
osfur

Ayn

عصفور

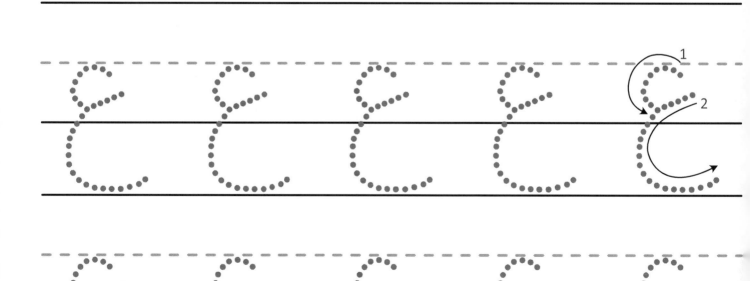

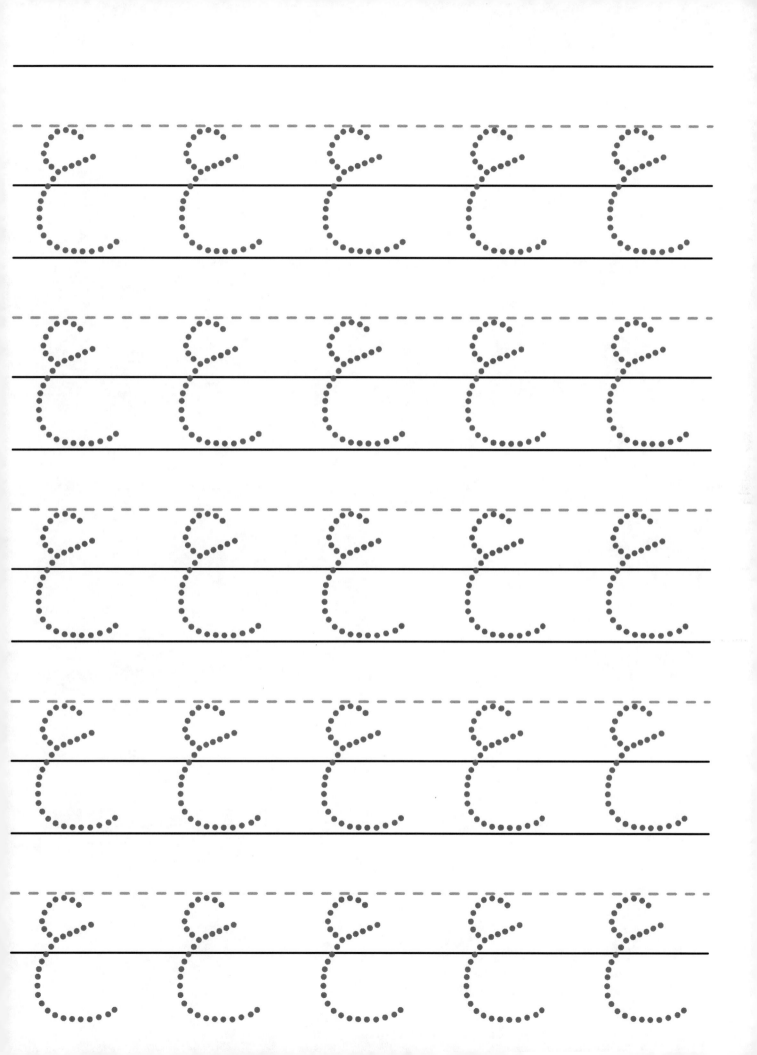

Deer
ghazal

Ghayn

غزال

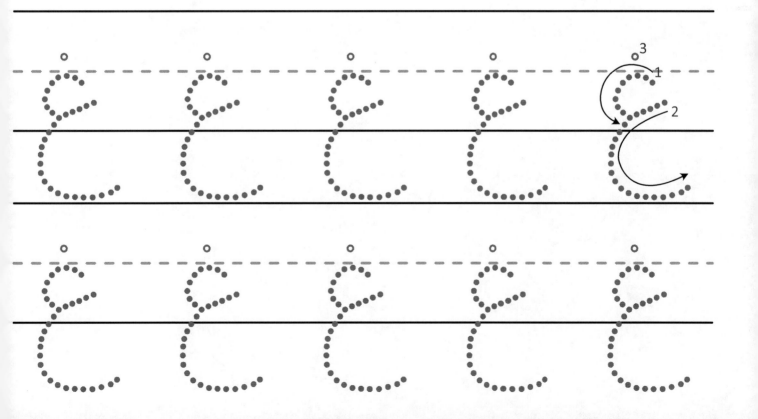

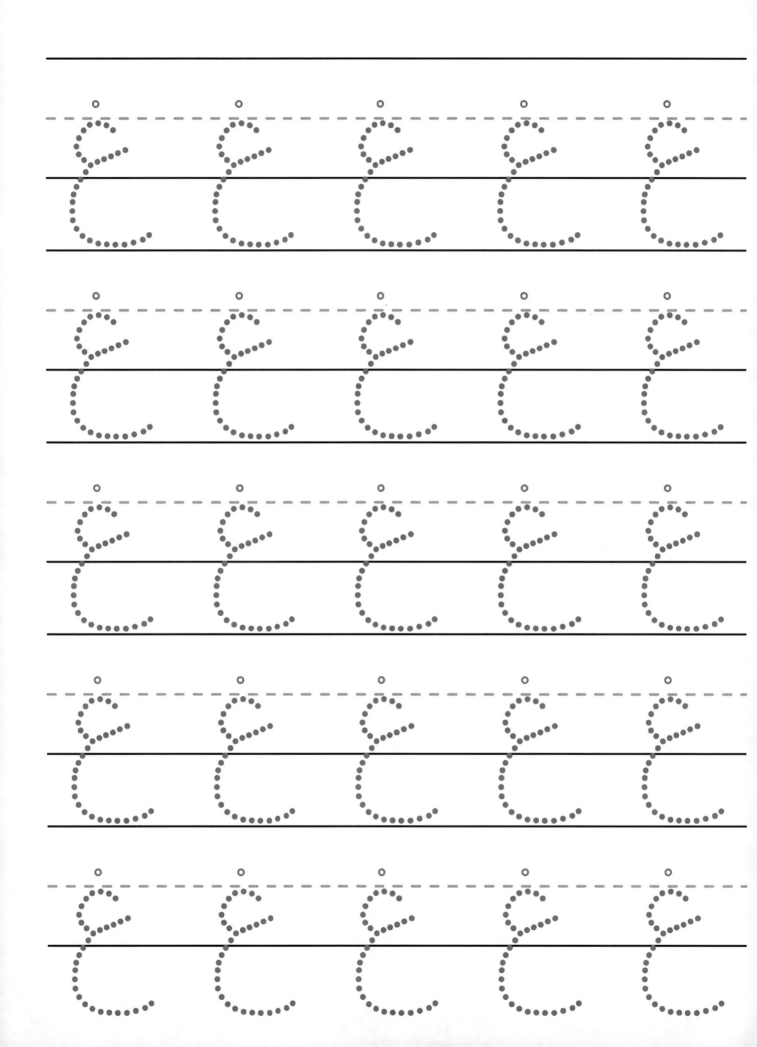

Mouse
faar

Faa

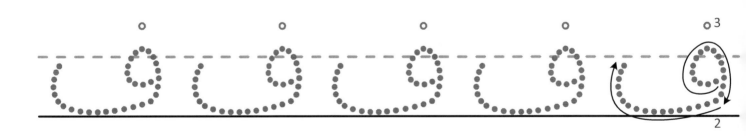

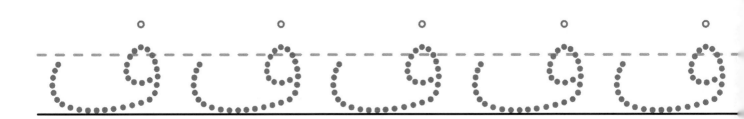

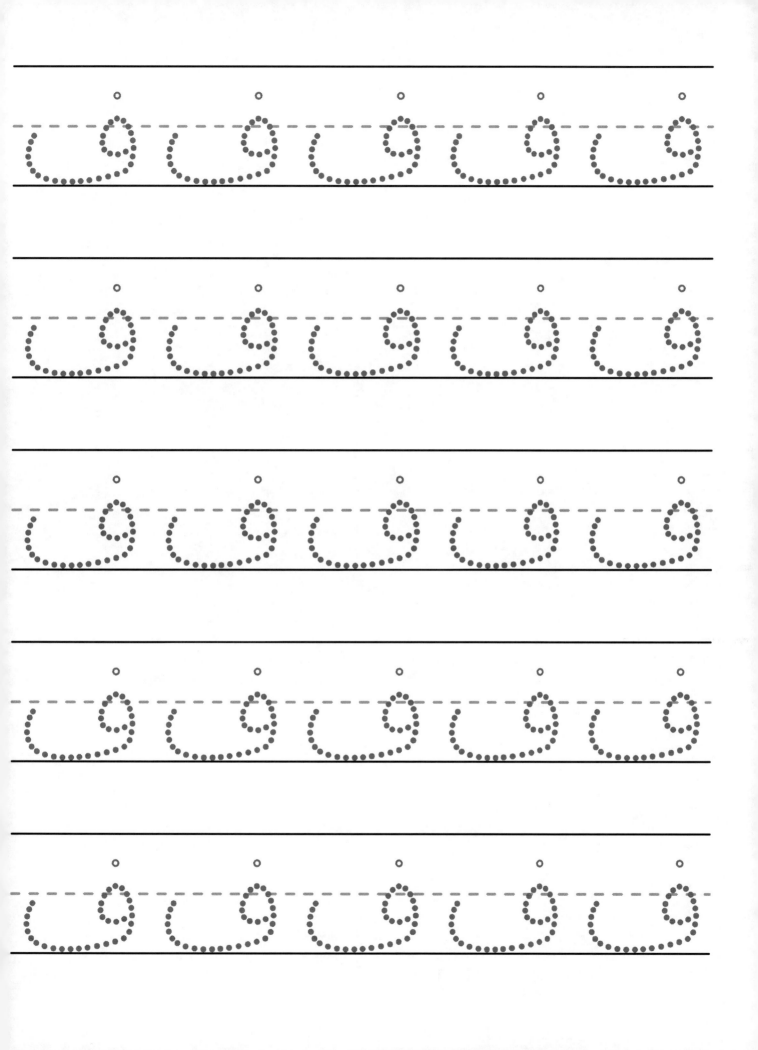

Train
qitar

Qaaf

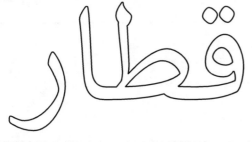

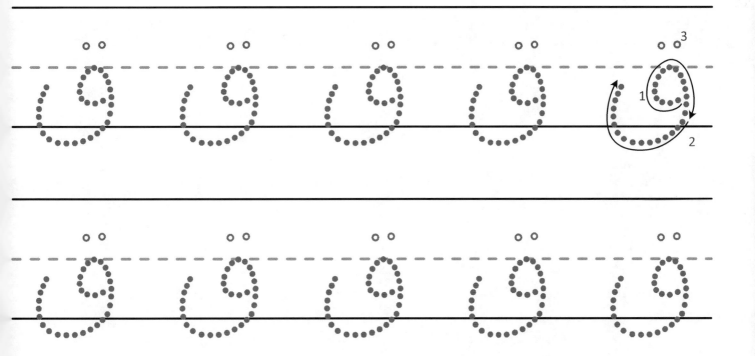

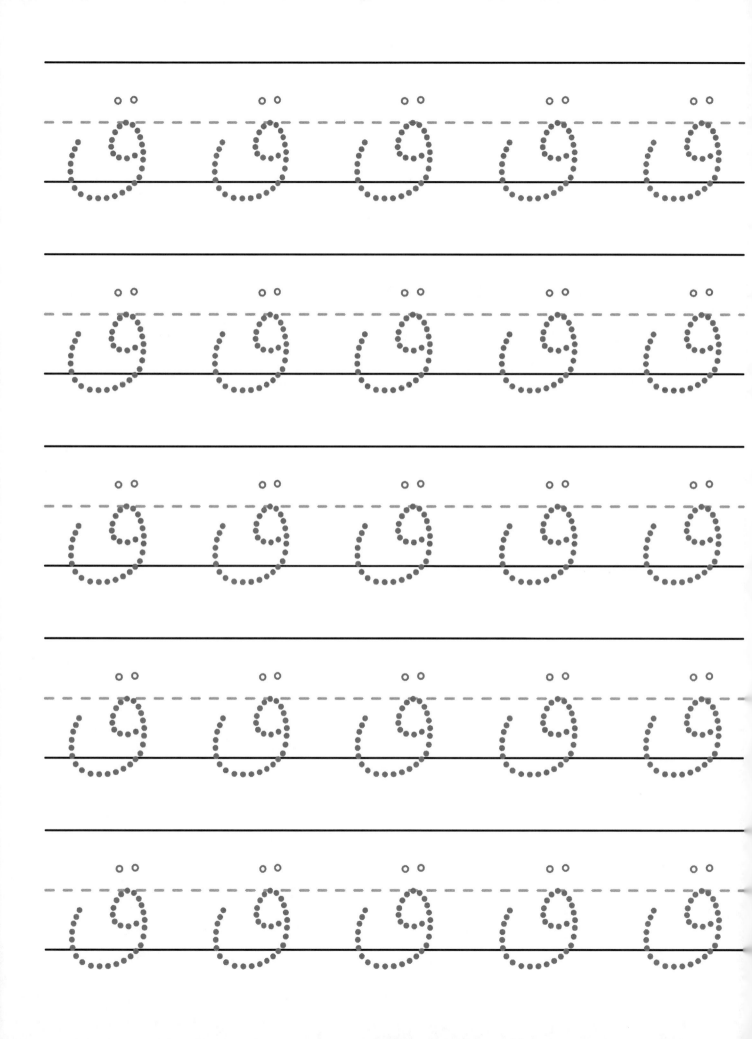

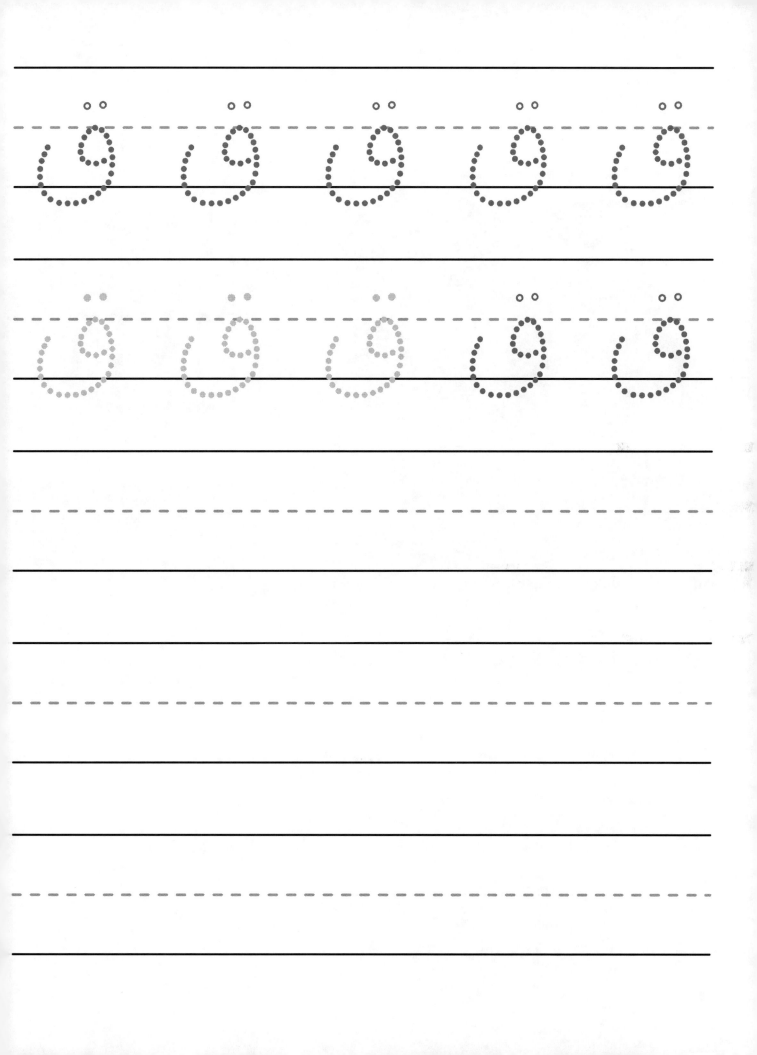

Cake
kaek

Kaaf

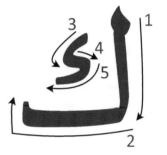

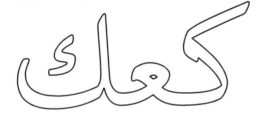

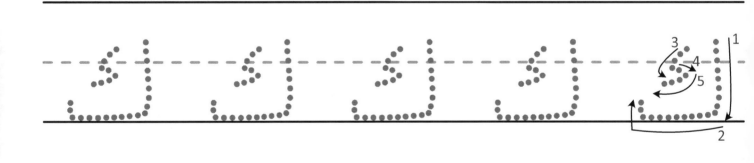

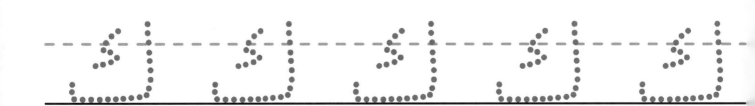

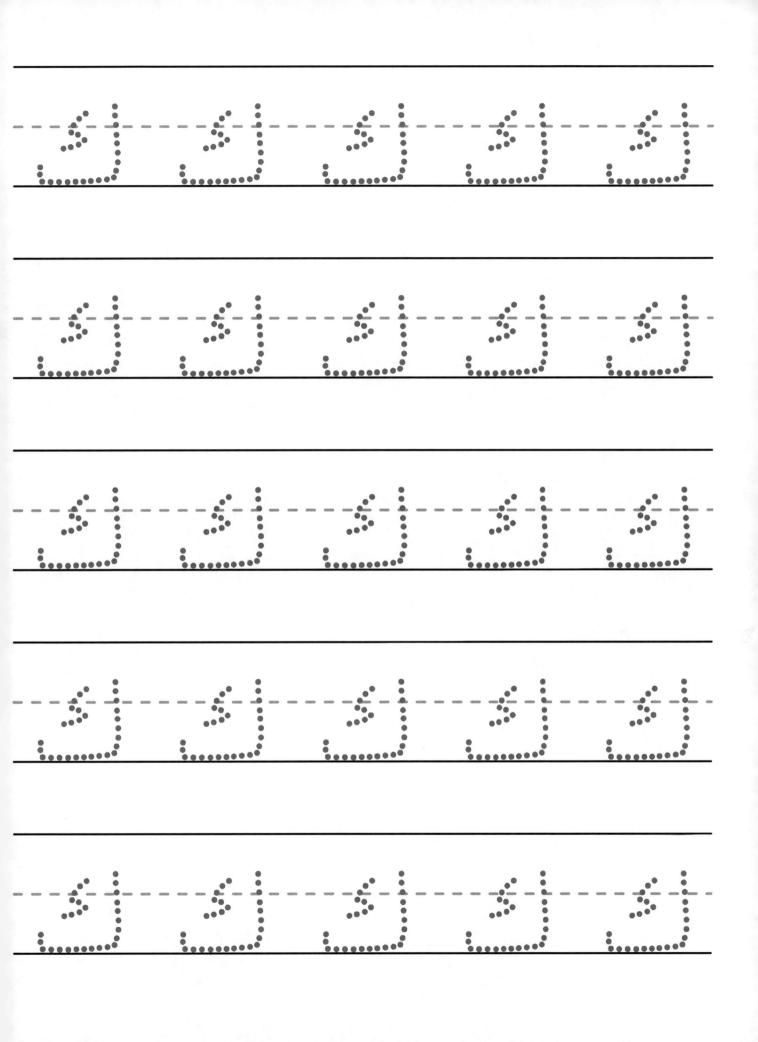

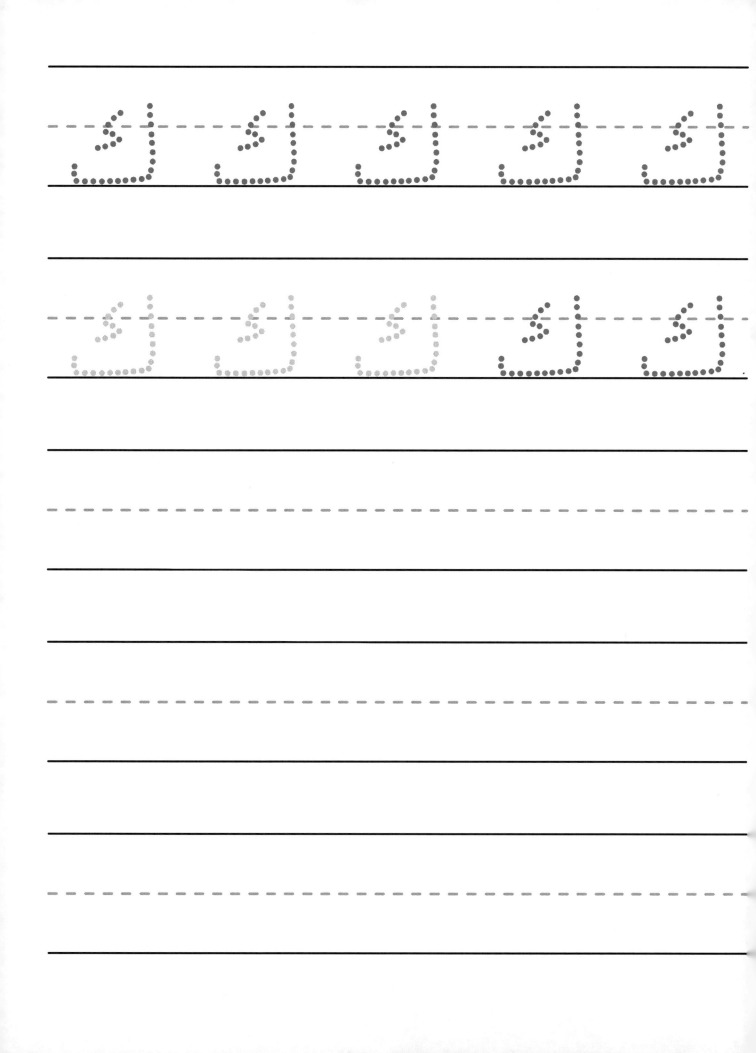

Laam

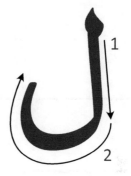

لعبة

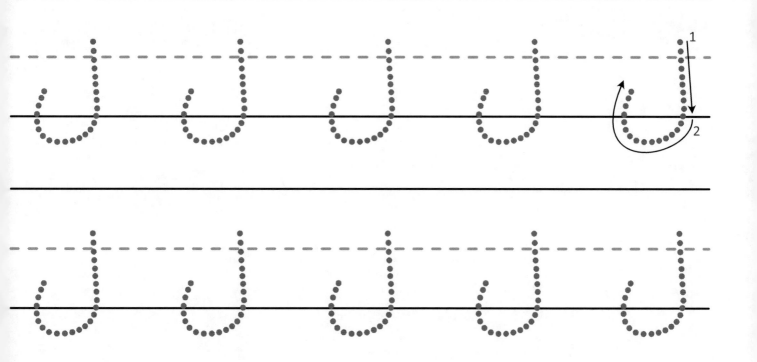

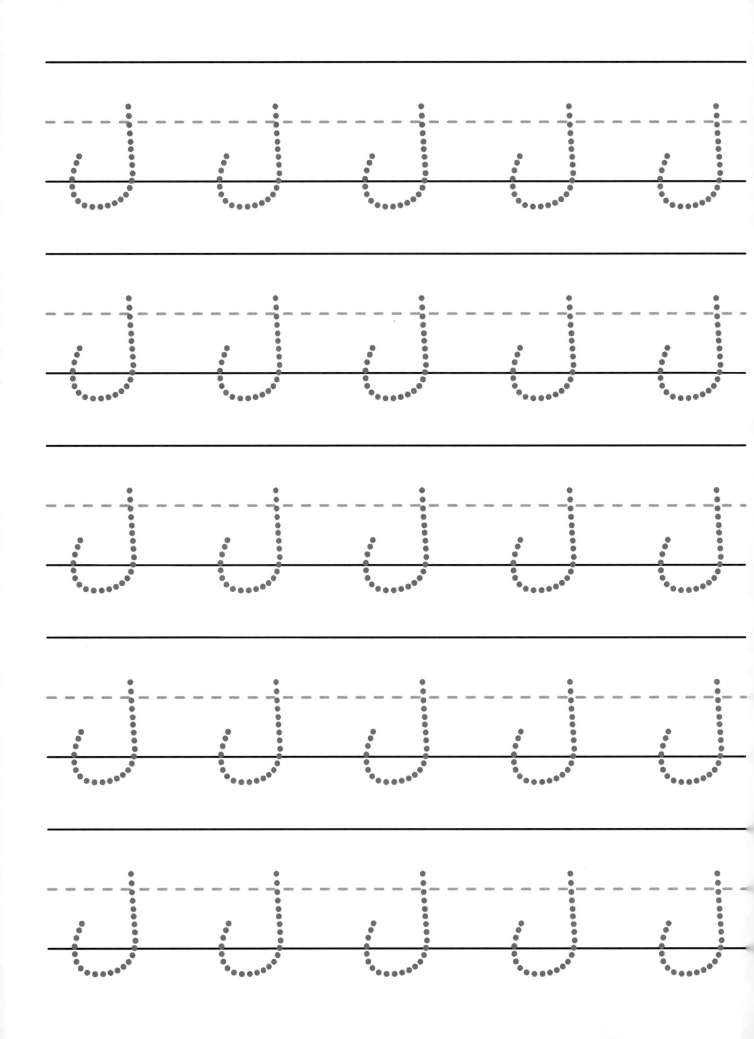

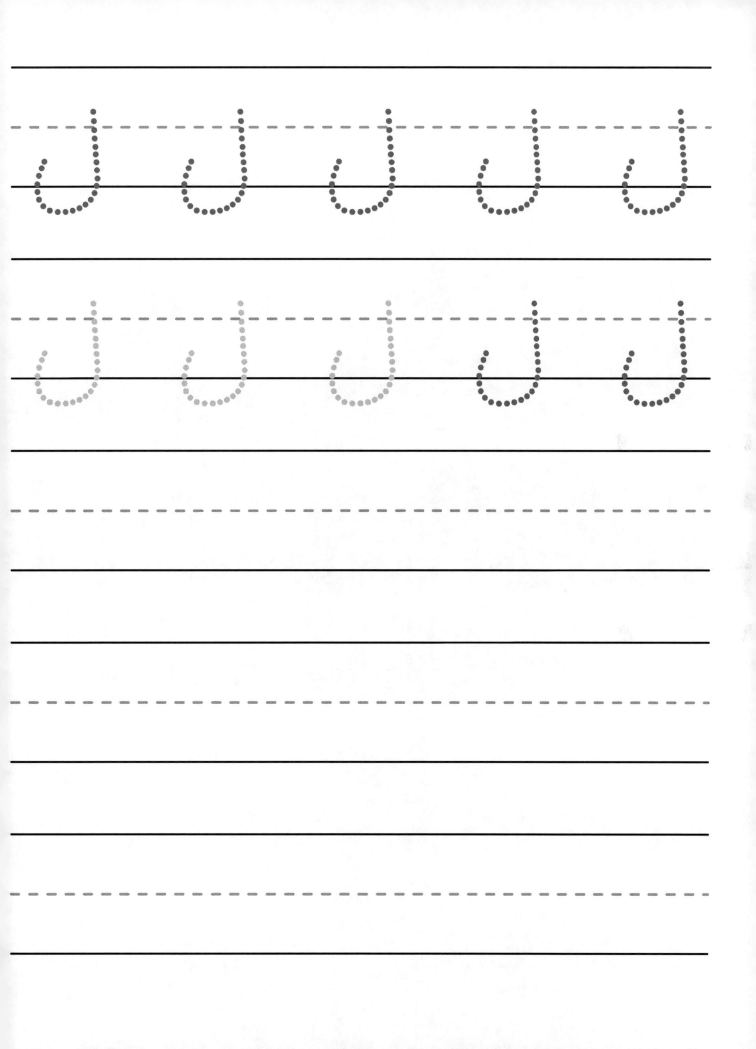

Meem

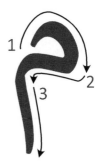

موز

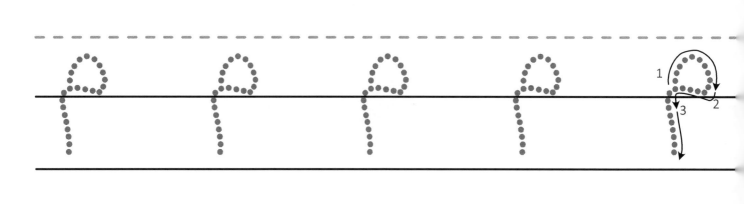

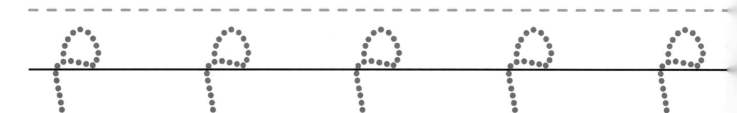

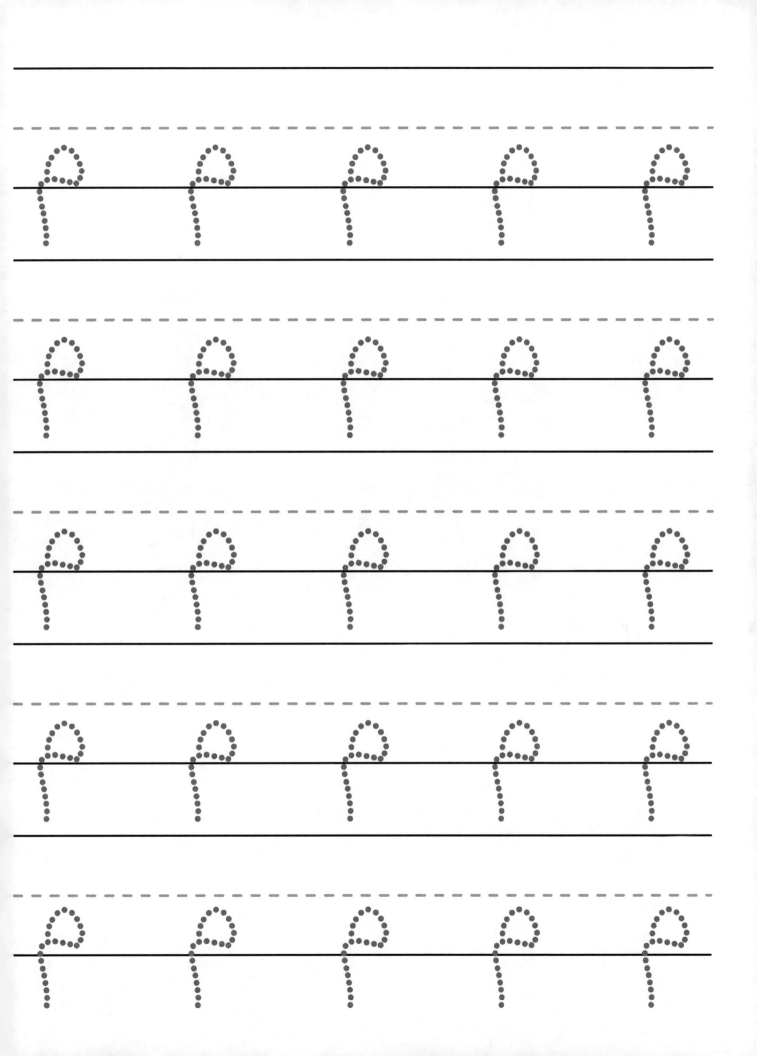

Tiger
namir

Noon

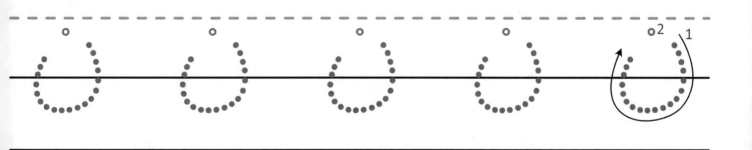

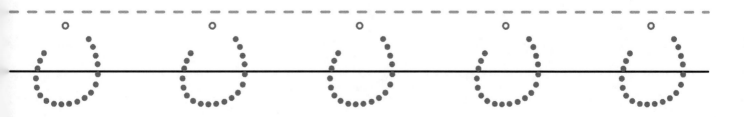

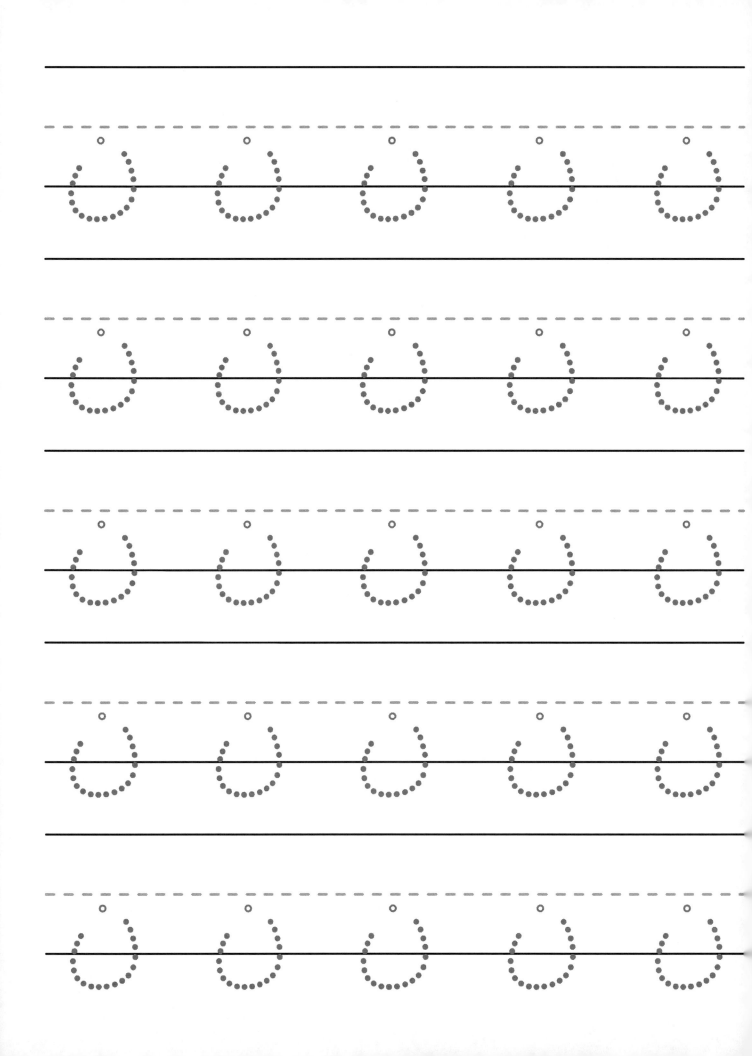

Phone
hatif

Haa

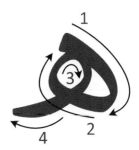

هاتف

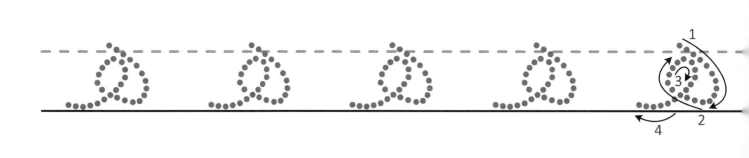

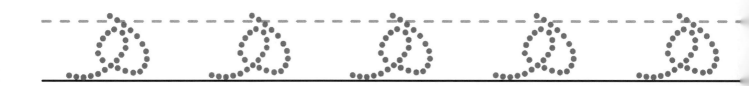

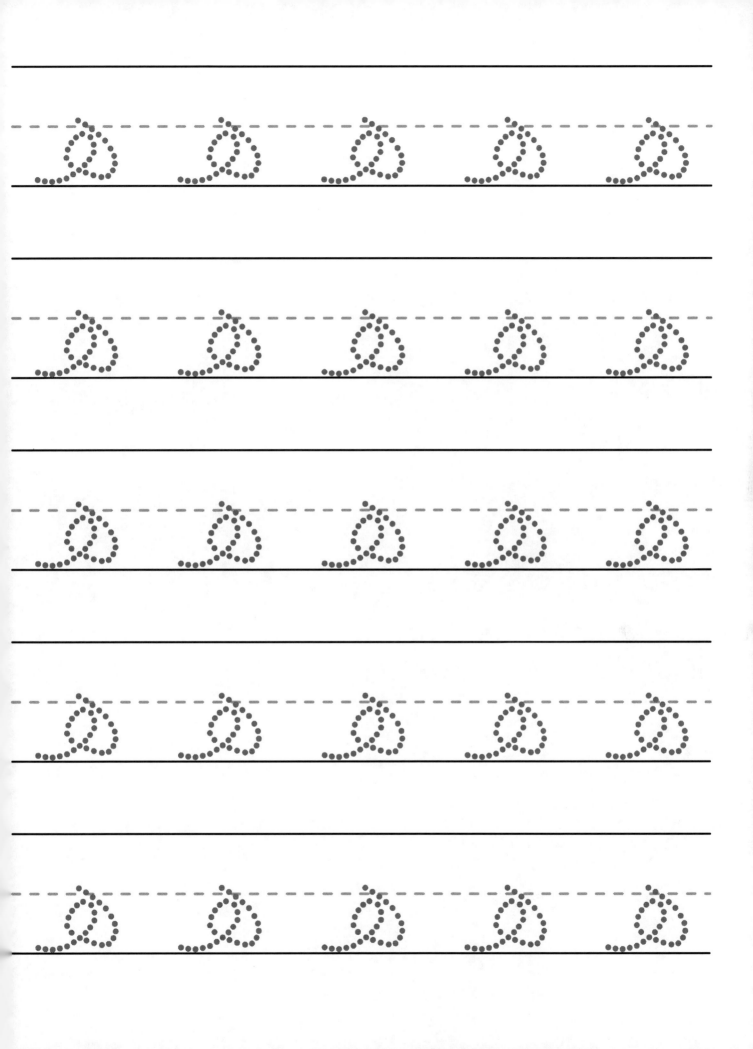

Pillow
wisada

Waaw

وسادة

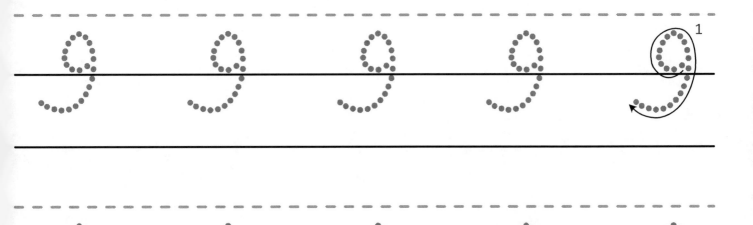

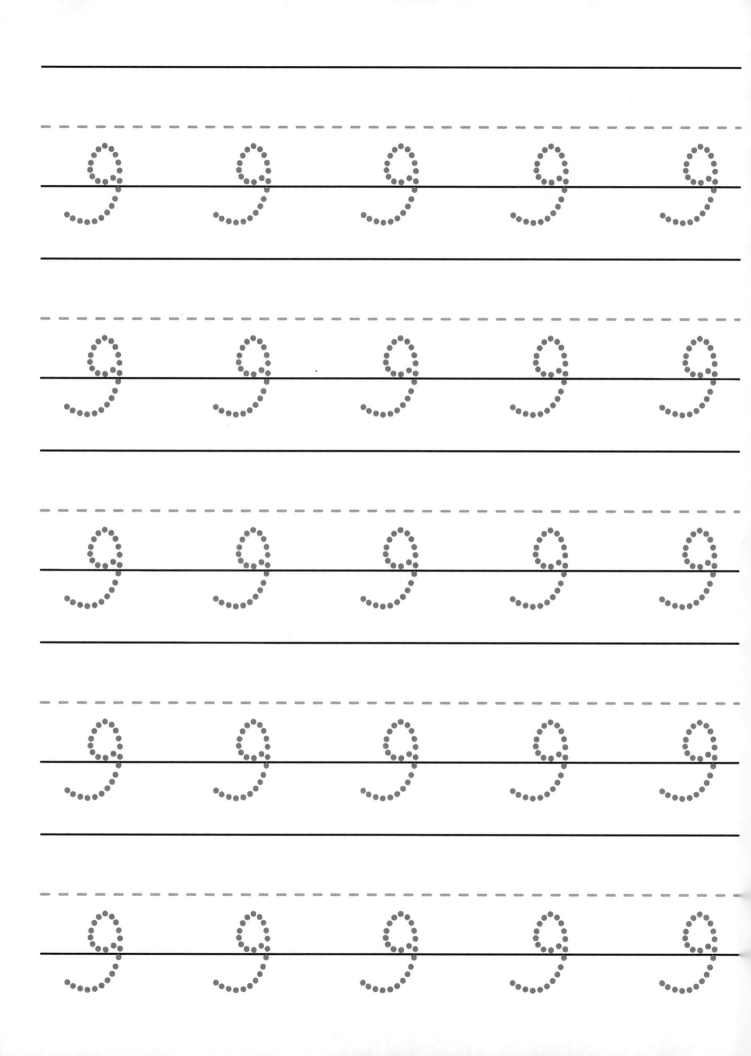

Pumpkin
yaqtin

Yaa

يقطين

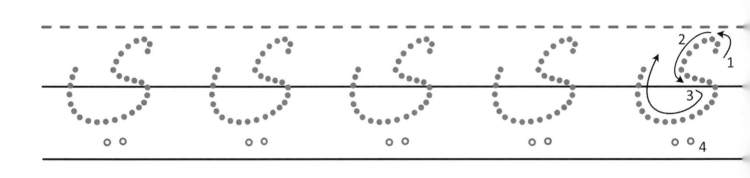

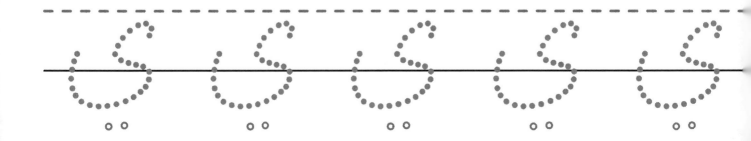

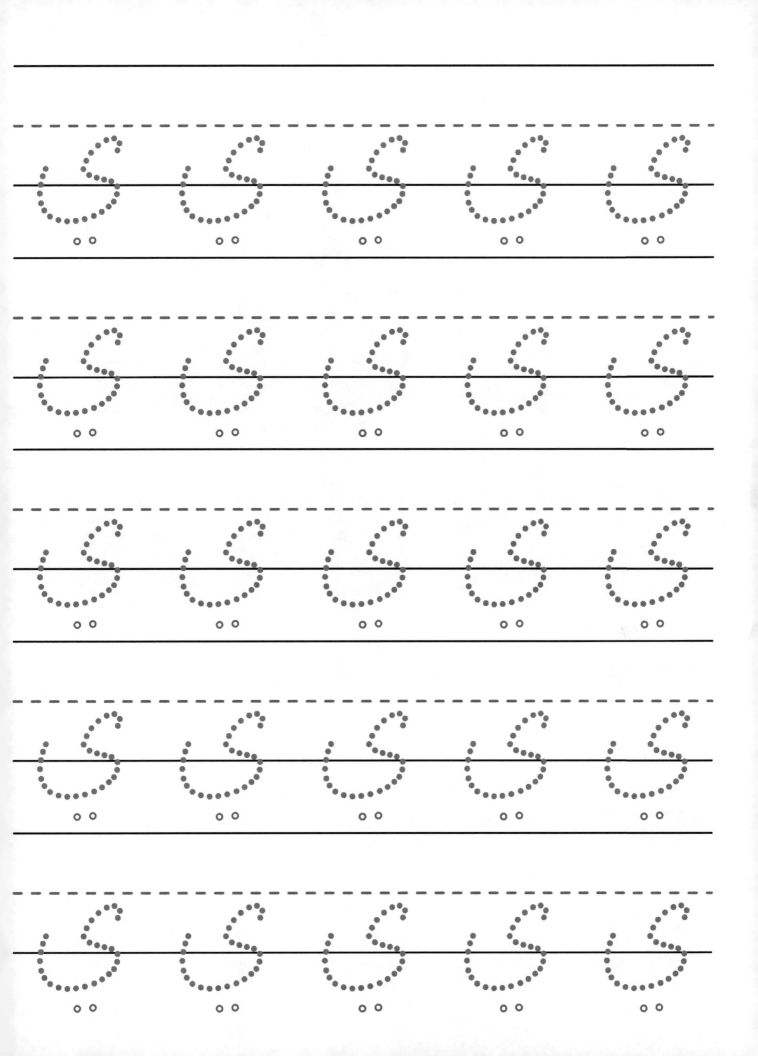

Made in United States
Troutdale, OR
03/13/2024

18428579R00051